THE POCKET TIMELINE OF
Ancient Rome

Katharine Wiltshire

OXFORD
UNIVERSITY PRESS

Published in association with The British Museum

Published in the United States of America by
Oxford University Press, Inc.
198 Madison Avenue
New York, NY 10016
www.oup.com

Oxford is a registered trademark of Oxford
University Press, Inc.

Oxford University Press, Inc., publishes works
that further Oxford University's objective of
excellence in research, scholarship, and
education.

Library of Congress Cataloging-in-Publication
data is available

ISBN-13:   978-0-19-530130-4
ISBN-10:   0-19-530130-7

Designed and typeset by Peter Bailey
for Proof Books
Printed in China

Illustration acknowledgements
All photographs are © the Trustees of the British
Museum, taken by the British Museum Photography
and Imaging Dept, unless otherwise stated.

The Bridgeman Art Library: Timeline (St. Peter's in
Rome), Ken Welsh / www.bridgeman.co.uk
Corbis: p.17 bottom (and Timeline), Jason Hawkes;
p.31 top (and Timeline), Archivo Iconografico, S.A.
Hadrian's Wall Tourism Partnership: p.27 top, Photo:
Graeme Peacock
Lesley and Roy Adkins: p. 8 top, p. 10 bottom, p. 13
bottom (and Timeline), p. 20 bottom (and Timeline),
p.31 bottom (and Timeline).
Peter Clayton: p. 6 bottom (and Timeline),p.18 top
(and Timeline)
Robert Harding: p. 23 top (and Timeline), p.30

ABOUT THIS BOOK

The story of ancient Rome takes place over
a period of more than 1000 years. During
this time Rome grew from a small village
to a mighty city ruled by kings, then a
republic, and later a vast empire.

This book will help you to find out more
about both the history of Rome and some
key aspects of Roman life such as villas,
towns and writing. These themed sections
are placed throughout the book and tell
you about things that were important to
the Romans, many of which existed
throughout the Roman period.

The timeline at the end of the book
provides you with more detailed dates for
specific events and general trends in
Roman history.

CONTENTS

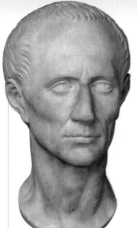

EARLY ROME

C. 2000 TO 616 BC

Between 2000 and 1000 BC, people began to settle near the River Tiber on the Italian peninsula. These people were farmers, who built their small settlements on the Palatine and Esquiline hills close by the river. The buildings in these villages were made of wood and had wattle-and-daub walls and thatched roofs. One of the main trading routes across the Italian peninsula at this time ran across the River Tiber near these villages, and as a result they grew wealthy from trade. During the 8th century BC, the villages on the hills joined together to become a single settlement. This settlement gradually became larger and developed into a town. This town was Rome.

A pottery model of a simple village hut.

This coin shows the mythical founders of Rome, the brothers Romulus and Remus, who, so the story goes, were looked after by a she-wolf.

ROMAN MONEY

BEFORE THE INVENTION of coinage, wealthy Romans stored their wealth in the form of copper ingots. These ingots each weighed about 1.5 kilograms (3⅓ lb)and were marked with symbols and pictures. Then, around 300 BC, the Romans copied the Greek idea of using coins and started to produce their own coinage. As well as being used to store wealth, coins were also used for buying and selling objects and labour. Roman coins were made from gold, silver and bronze.

During the Imperial Period, Roman coins usually had a picture of the emperor on one side, although sometimes it was another member of the imperial family, such as the emperor's wife. On the other side of the coin there was usually a picture. This was often a piece of imperial propaganda commemorating a great victory, peace across the empire, or just saying that the emperor was a strong, peaceful or just ruler.

A coin with the portrait of Faustina II, who was the daughter of the emperor Antonius Pius and wife of the emperor Marcus Aurelius.

An early form of Roman money. This bronze bar is marked with an elephant on one side and a pig on the other.

ROYAL ROME

A wall painting
showing Etruscan
people.

THE EARLY ROMAN villages on the hills near the River Tiber were ruled by individual village leaders. It was not until the villages became one settlement that they had a single ruler.

The first forum in
Rome was built by the
Etruscan king Tarquin.

The early settlement at Rome was influenced by its neighbours, the Sabines, and Rome itself was ruled by both Roman and Sabine kings. Then, in the 7th century BC, Tarquin I (who reigned from 616 to 579 BC) took control of Rome and turned it into a city. From 616 to 510 BC, Rome was ruled by members of the Tarquin family.

The Tarquins were Etruscans, who came from the region north of Rome where they lived in a number of cities, each ruled by its own king. Rome's position at a bridging point on the Tiber gave the Etruscans access to Latium and other regions to the south of their city-states. The Etruscans introduced writing to the Romans, although the Romans kept their own language. Stone foundations for buildings and tiled roofs date from this period. At the same time, a marshy area of land between the hills was drained. This was to become Rome's forum and it was laid out as a public square, which acted as a formal centre for the city. There was also a palace, temples and a city wall, known as the Servian Wall. The earliest recorded bridge in Rome was the wooden Pons Sulpicius, which was built across the River Tiber in the 6th century BC.

A richly decorated Etruscan water jug from around 500 BC.

This seated figure of *c.* 600 BC wears distinctly Etruscan clothing and jewellery.

ROMAN VILLAS

IN THE COUNTRYSIDE, villas formed the centre of farming estates surrounded by cultivated fields, meadows and forest. Villas produced and processed food, timber and animal products, such as leather and wool. Some large villas included a pottery, a mill or a blacksmith's forge. The Romans also used the word 'villa' to mean a holiday home near the sea or in the mountains.

The principal rooms in a villa would be heated by a 'hypocaust' system. A furnace drove hot air under the floors of the rooms, which were raised off the ground on stacks of tiles or piles of stones.

Inside the villa building, passages led from the main reception rooms to the living quarters. The important rooms often had mosaic floors and were decorated with wall paintings. Other villa rooms might include a library, a study and a bath-house. In some villas one room may have had a religious function. For example, at Lullingstone Villa, in southern England, part of the house was a shrine to three water goddesses, while at a later date some of the rooms were converted into a Christian house-church.

Part of the wall of a building from a villa estate in southern England, dating from the early 4th century AD.

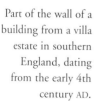

A wall frieze from Lullingstone Villa. This frieze comes from a room that may have been used as a place of Christian worship in the 4th century AD.

Large farming villas needed many people to run the land. Some worked in the fields while others looked after the animals, prepared grain, made cheese and so on. Others, such as secretaries, clerks and scribes, kept records of all the things the villa owner grew, bought or sold. These records were used to work out how much tax the villa owner had to pay, in grain or money, to the government. Those who lived in a town, away from their villas, usually hired a steward to be in charge and supervise all the people working on the estate.

The main rooms of a villa were often decorated with wall paintings, such as this coastal scene from a villa in Italy.

ROMAN RELIGION

PEOPLE FROM ACROSS the Roman world worshipped hundreds of different gods and goddesses. In Imperial times, even the emperor was worshipped as a god. Many Roman provinces had their own gods and goddesses. As these provinces became part of the empire, their gods and goddesses were absorbed into Roman religious practices. For example, at Bath, in southern England, the local god Sul was combined with the Roman goddess Minerva and was worshipped at a temple built near a hot-water spring, which had been sacred long before the Romans arrived in Britain. One important set of gods were the Greek Olympian gods, who were adopted by the Romans and linked to the gods they already worshipped. For example, Zeus and Hera, the king and queen of the Olympian gods, were associated with the Roman Jupiter and Juno.

Head of the god Mercury from the Roman temple dedicated to him at Uley. The head was probably part of a statue of the god that was set up inside the temple.

The Pantheon in Rome was built for all the unknown gods who otherwise would not have a temple dedicated to them.

The Romans built temples to their most important gods. People went to the temples to pray to the gods, to make offerings to them and to take part in religious festivals. In private houses there would often be small shrines used for worshipping household gods, known as the *lares*, and honouring family ancestors. The Romans believed that the *lares* helped to protect them. Private altars to household gods have also been found in some shops.

During the reign of the emperor Tiberius (AD 14–37), the Christian faith, based on the teachings of Jesus Christ, began to spread across the empire. Early Christians were frequently persecuted for their beliefs because they refused to worship the emperor. Then, in AD 313, the emperor Constantine the Great ordered that there should be complete freedom to worship all religions, including Christianity. However, it was not until AD 392, under the emperor Theodosius, that Christianity became the official religion of the Roman empire. All the temples to the Roman gods and goddesses were closed and twelve years later, in AD 404, a Latin version of the Christian Bible was completed.

The chi-rho symbol was used by early Christians. It consists of the first two letters of Christ's name in Greek. This wall painting from Lullingstone Villa also shows the letters alpha and omega, which were another early Christian symbol.

This gold medallion shows the emperor Constantine at prayer. He made Christianity one of the official religions of the Roman empire.

REPUBLICAN ROME

This early Roman coin dates from the time of the Roman republic. Instead of a portrait of a king or emperor, the coin shows the legendary Greek hero Herakles.

IN 510 BC, THE REIGN of the last king of Rome came to an end. Rome then became a republic ruled by an assembly of leading Roman citizens known as the senate. The senate was the place where matters of state were discussed and laws were passed. Each year two consuls, chosen from among the senate's members, were elected to rule as heads of government. The two consuls served for one year and were advised by the senate. In 494 BC the ordinary Roman people formed their own assembly, known as the *concilium plebis*, to represent their interests. This assembly worked under the senate, to help govern the city. Then in 451 BC the senate passed a series of written rules, known as the Twelve Tables, which recognized certain rights and gave the people of Rome their own representatives, known as tribunes. It was only later, in the 4th century BC, that ordinary people were allowed to be elected as consuls.

The chariot stadium in Rome, the Circus Maximus, was rebuilt in 174 BC. In this scene from a race, the chariot is just about to make a turn at three pointed columns, which mark the end of the central barrier.

By the 5th century BC Rome had become an important city. And as Rome grew more powerful and wealthy it began to extend the area it controlled by establishing settlements of Roman citizens (known as colonies) in the lands around the city. It even began to take control of some of the Etruscan cities that had once ruled Rome. Then, in 390 BC, Celtic people from Central Europe captured the city of Rome and destroyed it. The Romans rebuilt their city and provided it with better defences by rebuilding the city wall.

This is an Etruscan drinking cup. As the Romans expanded their territory, they took control of the Etruscan cities that had once ruled them.

After this setback, the Romans again began to expand into the surrounding regions of Italy. During the Samnite Wars (343–290 BC) against the powerful Samnite people of central Italy, the Romans managed to extend their control across to the Adriatic Sea on the other side of Italy. Eventually Rome controlled the whole of the Italian peninsula, either through political alliances or direct conquest.

The Via Appia was the first major road constructed in Rome. It was built in 312 BC.

This coin, minted in about 230 BC, shows one of the elephants used in the Carthaginian leader Hannibal's campaign against Rome during the Punic Wars.

Rome also began to take control of land beyond the Italian peninsula. During the Punic Wars (264–146 BC) against Carthage, a powerful city in North Africa, Rome won control of the island of Sicily, its first overseas territory. Rome's eventual victory in these wars gave it control in North Africa and the land around the western Mediterranean Sea. The defeat of Greece, in 146 BC, opened up the eastern Mediterranean and meant that Rome now controlled most of the region.

From about 150 BC, as Rome's territory grew in size and wealth, various powerful people tried to take control of Rome. Then, in 44 BC, the Roman general Julius Caesar took over as sole ruler. Many politicians in the senate were worried that Caesar would make himself king of Rome. As a result, he was assassinated in March 44 BC and the republic entered a period of unrest that ended only when Caesar's great-nephew, Octavian, won control of Rome and all its territory in 31 BC. Octavian became sole ruler and the Roman republic came to an end.

A plaque showing a Roman couple, Lucius Antistius Sarculo (on the left) and Antistia Plutia (on the right). They lived during the Republican and on into the Imperial period of Roman history.

ROMAN MOSAICS

AS EARLY AS THE 6th century BC, patterned floors were being made in Greece from natural coloured pebbles. However, true mosaics, made from coloured stone blocks, did not appear in Greece and Sicily until the 3rd century BC. Roman mosaics are made of small cubes called *tesserae*. These *tesserae* were shaped from stones of different colours.

Some mosaics featured geometric patterns, while others showed pictures inside a patterned border. Geometric designs were usually based on simple repeating patterns of lines or shapes. Picture mosaics were entirely different and might show gods and goddesses or animals – real and mythical. Pattern books were used to help design these mosaic floors. Complicated picture mosaics were often made in a special workshop ready to be laid all in one piece.

Mosaic floors have been found across the Roman world. In late antiquity, mosaics were also used as decoration for walls and ceilings and they became very popular in early Christian churches.

A floor mosaic from a villa at Hinton St Mary, in England. The face in the middle of the mosaic is believed to be the earliest portrayal of Christ in the Roman empire. It dates from the 4th century AD.

This mosaic is decorated with repeating geometric patterns.

THE ROMAN ARMY

THE ROMAN ARMY was made up of legions and auxiliary regiments. A legion consisted of about 5,000 foot-soldiers commanded by a senior officer called a *legatus*. Legionnaires were all Roman citizens. Each legion was organized into ten cohorts, which were further divided into centuries. Each century consisted of about eighty soldiers commanded by a centurion. The legions were highly trained and well equipped. Legions were sent out under the command of generals to conquer new territory with the aim of extending the Roman world. They were also responsible for building roads, forts and bridges.

Alongside the legions were the auxiliary regiments made up of 500 or 1,000 soldiers. Each regiment was commanded by a Roman officer. As with the main army, auxiliary regiments were divided into cohorts (commanded by a prefect) and centuries (commanded by a centurion). Auxiliaries were not Roman citizens. On leaving the army auxiliary soldiers were granted Roman citizenship.

A statue of a Roman legionary. Roman soldiers served for twenty-five years. At the end of this service they were granted full Roman citizenship and a parcel of land.

A bronze diploma issued to a Roman soldier called Marcus Papirus on 8 September AD 79. The diploma granted him and his family full Roman citizenship.

When Roman soldiers finished a day's march they would put up a camp as a temporary fortification overnight. In contrast, forts were permanent bases for the Roman army. The first Roman forts in an area were made of wood. Later they were rebuilt in stone. Most forts were constructed in the same way. They were usually rectangular in shape with rounded corners. The fort itself was surrounded by a wall and a ditch. Roads ran into the fort through gateways in each side of the wall. These roads met at a crossroads in the middle of the fort and at the centre stood the legion's headquarters. Other buildings included houses for the commander and senior officers, workshops, store-rooms, stables, baths, toilets and a hospital. Rows of barracks where the soldiers lived and slept stood on either side of the central buildings.

A decorative tile made in the tile workshop of the 20th Roman legion. The tile is decorated with the legion's emblem – the wild boar. The tile was probably made for one of the buildings at the legion's fortress.

Housesteads Roman Fort was built as part of the defences along Hadrian's Wall in northern England.

ROMAN TOWNS

TOWNS WERE A KEY FEATURE of any Roman territory. They served as the centre for local government and the market place for the surrounding area. The Romans often created towns when they took over control of new territory. For example, one of the first things the Romans did when they made Britain a Roman province was to build the town of Colchester (which was known as Camulodunun to the Romans) on the site of an earlier Roman fort.

Towns were governed by an *ordo* (council) of about a hundred people who were elected from among the town's citizens. Two pairs of magistrates were elected from the *ordo*, one pair to be in charge of justice in the town and the other pair to supervize public buildings and facilities.

The town of Pompeii, Italy, was buried under a layer of volcanic ash and pumice in AD 79. Excavations over the last 200 years have revealed its streets, buildings and some of its inhabitants.

This double portrait comes from an excavated house in Pompeii. It may show the owners of the house.

A Roman town was divided up into rectangular blocks by rows of streets. At the centre of the town was the *forum* (market place). Around the forum would be government offices, law courts and temples. The central open area of the forum was used as a market place and as somewhere public gatherings were held. Every town had at least one public bath-house where people went to bathe, exercise, conduct business and meet their friends. By the 4th century AD there were nearly 1,000 public baths in Rome alone. Most cities and major towns would have an amphitheatre and a theatre, or a public space that could operate as either. People in cities and towns often lived in *insulae*, which consisted of multi-storey buildings with shops and workshops on the ground floor and apartments above.

By law, burials took place outside Roman towns. This is the tombstone of a young Roman woman, Volusia Faustina.

This stone head probably comes from a tomb situated by the road leading out of the Roman town of Lactodurum (modern Towcester), England.

19

IMPERIAL ROME

31 BC TO AD 476

IN 31 BC, OCTAVIAN became sole ruler of Rome. Four years later, in 27 BC, the senate granted Octavian the title of Augustus, making him the first Roman emperor. The senate continued to give advice about how the empire should be run but it was now under the control of the emperor. When Augustus died in AD 14, he passed the title of emperor on to his adopted son, Tiberius. Rome was ruled by emperors for the next 400 years.

Augustus was the first official emperor of the Roman empire.

The 1st and early 2nd centuries AD were a time of great building activity in Rome. Many emperors built new *fora* (public squares) adjoining the *Forum Romanum*. The last and largest was Trajan's Forum with law courts, libraries, government offices and a temple, together with an adjacent shopping centre and a tall column to celebrate Trajan's military victories.

The Romans were great builders. This aqueduct in Spain was built using layers of arches. Aqueducts carried water into towns and cities.

begun in the AD 70s, was the largest amphitheatre ever built by the Romans and could seat more than 60,000 people. Roman ideas about building were recorded by the architect and military engineer Vitruvius, who wrote ten books all about Roman architecture.

At the same time the Romans continued to expand the territory they controlled and built up a vast empire. Augustus made Egypt a Roman province in 31 BC, and the emperors after him added further territory to the growing empire throughout the 1st century AD. Some new provinces were gained by conquest, others by political agreement.

The Roman empire reached its greatest extent under the emperor Trajan (AD 98–117), when the Romans controlled territory in Europe, Africa and Asia. The next emperor, Hadrian (AD 117–138), consolidated the frontiers of the empire and after his reign there were only small additions to the territory controlled by the Romans. During the later part of the 2nd century the Romans found themselves defending the empire against pressure from people outside the empire.

The Roman empire was at its largest extent under the emperor Trajan.

ROMAN ENTERTAINMENT

THE MAIN PLACES OF ENTERTAINMENT in a Roman city or town were the amphitheatre, where gladiatorial games took place, and the theatre. Roman plays were often based on Greek plays. Comedies were popular, and the Roman playwright Plautus (*c.* 254–184 BC), who came from Umbria, wrote more than 130 comic plays. Music was performed as part of a play but musical concerts were also given, often in a little theatre called an *odeon*.

Audiences at gladiatorial games and theatre plays were often very large. For example, the theatre at Pompeii could hold more than 5,000 people while the Colosseum in Rome had room for over 60,000 spectators. Horse races and chariot races

This gladiator's helmet was found at Pompeii.

A model of a racing chariot. Originally there would have been two horses pulling the chariot.

were held in a stadium known as a circus. The Circus Maximus in Rome was the largest in the Roman empire, with more than 250,000 seats. It was enlarged in the 4th century AD to hold 350,000 spectators.

Rome, together with many other towns and cities, had public libraries where people went to read the works of Roman as well as other writers. The Roman poet Ovid (43 BC–AD 17) wrote an epic poem in fifteen books called *Metamorphoses*, which is about people who changed into animals and plants. The Romans were also keen to record their past and they wrote about the early history of the city and the emperors who later came to rule Rome and its empire. For example, Livy wrote a history of Rome that covered the period from Rome's legendary beginnings to the time of the emperor Augustus, and Suetonius wrote about the lives of twelve of the Roman emperors. Writers, such as Cirero and Pliny the Younger, published their letters for other people to read.

The Colosseum was begun during the reign of the emperor Vespasian and took ten years to build.

The Romans believed that creative thoughts were inspired by goddesses known as the muses. One side of this silver casket shows the muses of music and theatre.

Roman actors wore costumes and masks to show which character they were playing. This is a mask from a tragic play.

ROMAN RULERS
JULIUS CAESAR
(RULED FEBRUARY–MARCH 44 BC)

Julius Caesar began his career as a general in the Roman army. After his time as a general he began a political career, holding various public offices and being elected as a consul in 60 BC. Then, in 59 BC, he was appointed governor of northern Italy and southern France. As governor, he decided that he was going to conquer the whole of Gaul (modern France and Belgium) and make it part of the Roman world. This took him eight years to achieve. During the campaign he led two expeditions to Britain, in 56 and 55 BC, although Britain was not to become part of the Roman empire until AD 43. In February 44 BC, following a period of civil war between Julius Caesar and his rivals, Caesar had himself appointed permanent ruler of Rome. This worried many in the senate who thought that Caesar was about to declare himself king and so, on 15 March 44 BC, he was assassinated.

A marble bust of Julius Caesar.

A Samian-ware bowl. This type of pottery was first made in the Roman province of Gaul.

AUGUSTUS (REIGNED 31 BC–AD 14)

Octavian was the adopted son of Julius Caesar and became the first emperor of the Roman empire. He took control of Rome after a period of political unrest following the death of Caesar. In 27 BC the senate granted him the title of Augustus, and this is the name by which he is most commonly known. Augustus reformed the way in which the government worked and secured the frontiers of the empire, thereby bringing peace and stability to the Roman world. Augustus undertook much building work in Rome and constructed many public monuments. He also built a new forum to serve as a legal and administrative centre for the city and had many of the existing buildings in Rome faced with marble to give them a grander appearance.

Augustus was also a patron of the arts and his reign was a golden age for Roman literature with writers such as Horace, Virgil and Livy. When Augustus died, in AD 14, he passed the title of emperor on to his adopted son, Tiberius.

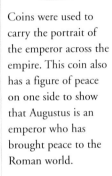

Coins were used to carry the portrait of the emperor across the empire. This coin also has a figure of peace on one side to show that Augustus is an emperor who has brought peace to the Roman world.

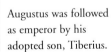

Augustus was followed as emperor by his adopted son, Tiberius.

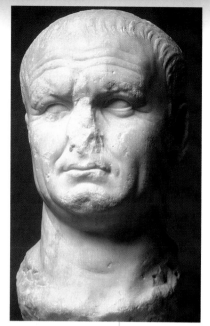

The emperor Vespasian.

This coin commemorates the opening of the Colosseum, which occurred during the reign of Vespasian's son Domitian.

VESPASIAN (REIGNED AD 69–79)

Vespasian's background was middle class. Before becoming emperor he had followed a public career as a tribune (a representative of the people), praetor (a judge), consul (one of the two annually elected heads of government) and finally a governor (someone in charge of a province). Vespasian began his imperial reign during a year of unrest following the death of the emperor Nero. During this year there were three other emperors – Galba, Otho and Vitellius – before him. Vespasian was initially proclaimed emperor in July AD 69 while he was in the eastern part of the empire in command of the eastern legions. At the same time, Vitellius, commander of the Rhine legions, was ruling as emperor in Rome. Vespasian returned to Rome where he defeated Vitellius and finally became undisputed ruler in December AD 69. He was followed as emperor, in turn, by his two sons Titus and Domitian.

HADRIAN (REIGNED AD 117–138)

Hadrian saw his role as consolidating, rather than expanding, the Roman empire and he travelled extensively around the empire. When Hadrian visited Britain in AD 122, he ordered the building of a stone wall across the north of the province to act as a frontier. This wall became known as Hadrian's Wall. Hadrian loved the culture and literature of Greece and he spent at least three winters in Athens where he had a library, a forum and an arch built. He visited Egypt in AD 130 and travelled up the River Nile as far as Thebes. Hadrian

built himself a wonderful palace at Tivoli near Rome, with beautiful buildings to remind him of different Roman provinces. The palace stretched for over 1.6 km (1 mile) and was set in ornamental gardens. In Rome itself Hadrian was responsible for the rebuilding of the Pantheon temple. When he died he was followed as emperor by his adopted son, Antoninus Pius.

Hadrian's Wall is 80 Roman miles long (117 km or 73 modern miles). It stretches across northern England.

This head comes from a statue of Hadrian, which was probably put up in the forum in London to commemorate Hadrian's visit to Britain in AD 122.

27

ROMAN PROVINCES

This letter from Vindolanda, near Hadrian's Wall, mentions the name of the governor of Britain. This reference helps to date the letter to around AD 95.

THE ROMANS GAINED their first overseas territory during the First Punic War of 264–241 BC. This territory was the island of Sicily, to the southwest of the Italian mainland. Later territory was added to the Roman world by direct conquest or through political agreement. Eventually, the Roman empire included provinces on three continents – Europe, Africa and Asia. These provinces brought Rome great prestige and wealth from trade. The provinces were also a source of food products. For example, the province of Africa supplied two-thirds of Rome's corn. New towns and cities with Roman-style bath-houses, temples and public *fora*, (the plural of forum), were built in the provinces and Roman citizenship was gradually extended to the people living in these

Cleopatra VII was the last independent ruler of ancient Egypt. After her death in 30 BC, Egypt became a province of the Roman empire.

towns and cities. People from the provinces soon joined the senate, and the emperors Trajan and Hadrian both came from Spanish families.

The territories that Rome controlled were ruled by Roman governors.

These governors commanded the troops and were responsible for local law and order. There was also a procurator for each territory, who was in charge of collecting taxes and paying the army. Both the governors and the procurators were chosen, at first, by the senate and later by the emperor. Each governor had a staff of slaves and military clerks to help him with his work.

Various provinces were famous for their own specialized goods. For example, Egypt was important for the vast quantities of grain that it grew; beautiful Samian-ware pottery was produced in Gaul; wine and marble were imported from Greece; and Spain was well known for its olive oil, fish sauce and cloth. The Romans were also keen to explore beyond their provinces. In AD 60 the emperor Nero sent an expedition to explore Meroe (Sudan) and in AD 166 an embassy from the emperor Marcus Aurelius reached China.

These burial goods, found at Welwyn Garden City, shows the amount of trade going on even before Britain became a Roman province.

In 133 BC the last king of Pergamum left the city to Rome. This coin from the city shows the emperor Augustus.

LATER ROME

This coin shows the Ostrogoth king Theodohad. He ruled one of the small kingdoms that emerged in Italy after the fall of the western Roman empire.

Rome is the capital city of modern Italy.

FROM AD 476 During the 3rd century AD, the Roman empire faced social, economic and political difficulties. So in order to make the empire easier to run, the emperor Diocletian (reigned AD 284–305) divided the empire into four regions, each with its own ruler. The empire was briefly reunified by the emperor Constantine (reigned AD 324–337), although in AD 395 the Roman empire was officially divided into a western and an eastern part and was never again ruled by a single emperor. During the 4th century AD, people from regions around the edge of the empire, such as the Vandals and the Visigoths, invaded the western empire and settled the land. The last emperor of the western empire, Romulus Augustulus, was overthrown in AD 476. After this, Italy fragmented into many small kingdoms and states. It was not until almost 1,400 years later, in AD 1870, that Italy was unified as one country. Nowadays, it is the Republic of Italy and it has its capital city at Rome.

The eastern part of the Roman empire was ruled from the city of Constantinople (the modern-day Turkish city of Istanbul). The emperor Heraclius (AD 610–641) changed the way in which the eastern empire was run and it became known as the Byzantine empire. The emperor Justinian I (reigned AD 527–565) won back control of some of the western empire including Italy, which had been overrun by Germanic tribes, and North Africa. However, by the AD 560s Justinian had lost control of most of this territory. The Byzantine empire grew smaller and weaker over the centuries and, in AD 1453, the Ottoman Turks conquered Constantinople and made it part of their Ottoman empire. The Ottoman empire ended in AD 1918 and the area that it formerly controlled now contains many different countries, such as Turkey, Syria and Jordan, each with its own government.

A mosaic showing the emperor Justinian and his court.

The church of St Sophia in Istanbul (Constantinople).

FURTHER READING

EVERYDAY LIFE IN ANCIENT ROME
Neil Grant
British Museum Press, 2004

LEGACIES FROM ANCIENT ROME
Anita Ganeri
Belitha Press, 2003

ILLUSTRATED ENCYCLOPAEDIA
OF ANCIENT ROME
Mike Corbishley
British Museum Press, 2003

EYEWITNESS GUIDE TO
ANCIENT ROME
Simon James
Dorling Kindersley, 1990

SOME USEFUL WEBSITES:
The main British Museum website can be found at
www.thebritishmuseum.ac.uk

COMPASS
COMPASS allows you to browse the British Museum's collections
on line, with thousands of images and background information
about objects and the people who made and used them. COMPASS
also features a wide range of tours about the Museum's exhibitions
and other themes.
www.thebritishmuseum.ac.uk/compass

CHILDREN'S COMPASS
There are hundreds of objects from around the world on Children's
COMPASS. Find out about different cultures from around the
world and compare key themes based around everyday life, belief,
technology and rulers.
www.thebritishmuseum.ac.uk/childrenscompass